Lullabies Through the Storm

a lavender littered path

Anushka Saha

ISBN

Hardcase 979-8-89322-916-5
Paperback 979-8-89277-340-9

To dada, papa and mumma.

Contents

Introduction to the Author

Anushka Saha is an Indian poet who holds a Master's degree in English Literature with Communication studies from Christ University, Bangalore. She began writing poetry about unicorns and puppies at the age of 9. As she grew older her poetry began to address more complex themes.

During her Bachelors she was introduced to the art of confessional poetry and having found solace in the works of Anne Sexton and Sylvia Plath, she learnt to channel her experiences into written and spoken word. The women that wrote before her allowed her to find comfort in their words, and now she wishes to pay it forward. Saha strongly maintains that trauma is a word as heavy as the consequences of enduring it, and having experienced it firsthand, she writes about everything it came to her with. Her personal trysts with abuse, grief and suffering have helped shape her writing into what it is today. Every poem is different and voices the struggles of a different woman, highlighting the severity of what they face.

Her poetry is for women that require shelter, a space where their struggles aren't shrugged off as unimportant or simply too graphic to be talked about. Having grown up reading fiction that she believes walked her through the sunlit gardens and quagmires of her adolescence, she wishes to give back to the medium that saved her.

The poems included in this book provide a glimpse of her writing style and all the subjects she cares about. They are a reflection of how she perceives the world and what beliefs she houses to be able to function in it. As a poet she is constantly looking for ways to improve her poetry, to make it more impactful. Her dedication and drive help contribute towards making her a well-rounded writer, well on the path to writing better poems and telling better stories.

The Weight of a Pound of Flesh

I used to sit on my little pink chair,
And at the night sky I would stare.
Hoping shooting stars would fall to their demise.
Just so I could whisper a prayer,
One beautiful verse for the night
A ritual to ease my plight.
My religion, a dimming beacon of light.

Fairies lurking behind the turquoise skies
Would hear my half hearted cries and
Fly down to my windowsill,
Holding out their hands, smiles awry.
Cradled in each palm,
Would lie a sliver of silver.
A star that shattered,
Bidding the heavens goodbye.

One Autumn morning,
As the sunlight shone upon my window pane,
My Baba smiled down at me
And I knew,
The stars had heard my plea.
My Baba was a happy man,
That's all that I would ever need.

The next Winter I found myself burying my innocence,
A deep chasm I carved inside of my chest.
As I sealed the coffin with pink satin,
All the fairies came to weep at its wake.
There's only so many times a girl can hear her father say,
"The faster you grow up, the better shona.
It would be a lot easier to marry you off that way."
As the sun retreated and dusk arrived
It dawned on me what I was supposed to do,
Become a bride and a mother of two.

As I outgrew my little pink chair,
The shackles around my wrists continued to morph.
At fifteen they were the sleeves that hid my scars,
At seventeen they became the henna that lined my arms.
Responsibilities my shoulders should never have had to bear,
Now sat with me at the altar square.
The names hidden in my mehendi,
Spelt out a lifetime of despair.

The garlands of Gulmohar
Had camouflaged themselves,
Hiding the grip of an ever tightening noose.

The bright amber of the flowers was but an
elaborate ruse.
Buried in a shallow grave of gold and vermillion
stained promises,
My dreams were never going to come true.

Baba placed a bounty on my chest,
And as the wedding shehnai played,
My womanhood was sold, wrapped in a crimson
lehenga,
A price attached to my being.
He didn't call it dowry,
And they would never use the word,
But I was just a commodity,
A price had always been a part of my worth.

A pawn in the gamble that was marriage.
A criminal who would never stop serving time,
Locked in a cage that I was forced to love.

Baba bought me the prettiest bribes,
Skirts tinged with azure and shiny glass bangles,
All to soften the blows.
If only he knew, my bruises would soon be
wrapped
In the same azure hues.

"The way to a man's heart lies in the sheets"
So I close my eyes and wait,

After a long, unhappy day,
To comfort him through my pain.
When he mistakes my whimpers for desire,
And crushes my waist with his weight,
I must remember to hold my breath, and play along,
For a good wife never lets her man down.

Looking at my tired arms now,
I yearn for what could have been.
The far fetched fantasy of a fairy realm.
A land where blankets are warm and soft,
Never shields to silence deafening screams.
Or bathed in the rust coloured rivulets of forced consent.

Is there a world where my ovaries are simple organs
And not factories that produce heirs to pacify a father's desires?
Is there a world where my knees aren't bleeding and bruised,
From kneeling in front of men that look like my fears,
Breaking my aching back,
By carrying the burdens of their sins.
And as all my ambitions lay shrivelled from doing their bidding,
I close my eyes and pray for a new beginning.

I'm afraid of my womb,
Scared for the life it will bring.
This part of my body that doesn't really belong to me,
Always pushing me to the brink.
A forsaken organ,
The repository for a man's desires.
This pound of flesh,
This ounce of meat,
Nothing but a symbol of forged consent.

Will the pink of my prison cell,
Stain the lives growing inside of me as well?

And when the months have passed
And I have bidden my time,
As my cries are drowned,
Will I have to watch as my little girl is bound?
When her destiny is etched in lines of henna,
That stain her dainty palms,
Do I have to stand by and watch?
Or will I find the courage to let out a forbidden scream?
An act of rebellion in the hopes of protecting her dreams.

As I stare at the night sky tonight,
Waiting for shooting stars to fall to their demise,
I must whisper a prayer,
A new one for this night.

A ritual,
A cry for help.
My religion,
And my very last attempt
At shattering the glass ceiling my Baba had so carefully built,
If only to lessen the crushing burden of carrying around this guilt.

The Urns That Line My Bedroom Shelves

I was born in a bankrupt brothel
To a woman who didn't know love.

Screams pierced the veil of the night,
And as the walls shrunk down on her legs that had been spread wide,
(Consensually, for the very first time)
Out came her biggest mistake, one in a long line.
Birthed from a lack of options,
I tore through my mother on that forsaken night.
She screamed bloody murder,
Praying I would just give up and die.
Blood caked her feet and trailed down her knees,
And there I was sobbing in the dimming light.
A picture that would foreshadow the rest of my life.

Seconds after entering the world,
I was drenched in blood, guts and gore.
Cradled by torn washcloth,
The prophecies predicted: this foetus was rotten to its core.

The love I was given hid behind vows of silence.
Contracts of confidentiality made my body a page
for the safe expression of violence.

When I would ask about my father
My mother told me he could be any man in a
crowd.
Perhaps even the ones that visit me on Friday
nights.
Romance was an elixir that wasn't for me to taste.
Aphrodite has abandoned this lane.
Love wouldn't survive here, nothing good ever does.

Churches don't let us in, so we fit our faith in a
basement.
Walls that were white are now smothered in gray.
Beds became pews for the faithful to pray,
A haven for the women that even the heavens
betrayed.
Candelabras cradle the ends of cigarettes,
Cracked chalices line the shelves.
A place of worship, a place of hope,
Breeding faithless women that were never given a
chance to cope.

My bedroom window was a meagre hole in the wall.
It overlooked a sea of dreams in a city lit up with
twinkling lights

And as they died out,
I'd look down and see the occasional condom lying on the ground.
Undisturbed, unwanted
And abandoned like the children its absence birthed.

I wonder what it's like when sex is an option,
An act of pleasure, not one of survival.
The memories come back when I least expect them,
Through whiffs of cheap liquor and dances of light.
Glint of gold watches dangling above me,
Flashing against the never ending night.
The kicks that landed square upon my bleeding shins,
The act of fulfilling an unfaithful man's fantasies of sin.
They'd all remind me of what the burden of a day's wage lay in.

"The blood of the coven is thicker than the water of the womb",
It seems fitting that the only family I have was brought together
Through the mistakes of the ones that came before us.
On the nights when we were too bruised to move,
My sisters and I would take turns telling stories

That would transport us to a world where we could live normal lives.
With home cooked meals and blanket forts we would build,
Under the soft bedroom light.
A home where our mothers had better lives,
With fathers who kissed us goodnight.

One cold July evening,
There were no stories left to tell.
Our sister succumbed to a lonely man's rage.
All she left behind was a tube of lipstick, a burnt scarlet.
And when her body went cold we painted her blue lips red,
In the moonlight they turned crimson.
A fitting end for a child of the red light realm.
At least she died painted in familiar hues,
The shades of blood that would bathe her sheets,
Strangled her to sleep too.
When we called the funeral homes to bury her body,
Finally allow her some rest,
A familiar man picked up and delivered what he believed was Divine Judgement.
We were forced to burn her in the basement instead.
In an urn our sister lay, a reminder of the world and its cruel ways.
The fireplace in our basement, turned into a funeral pyre overnight.

My sisters' urns line the shelves,
A reminder of my chosen family and the birthrights they were denied.
As my screams pierce the veil of the night,
And the walls shrink down on my legs that have been spread wide,
I pray I could just give up and die.
Blood cakes my feet and trails down my knees,
And there I sit sobbing in the dimming light.
After all, the prophecies were right.

The Cerulean Stained Secret

On moonlit July evenings
I sit on my beloved Jamun tree.
Hands resting against the bark where my name sits carved,
Looking at the cerulean waves of the sea.

The chill that haunts this winter night
Almost brings my fragmented soul back to life.
I'm nothing but a remnant now.
A memory, bare wisps of what once was.
Disembodied fragments held together by light,
A mere shadow birthed from treachery.

People shuffle past me
Consumed by the sins that haunted them before my body turned to dust.
The sand their feet sink into shifts and moulds,
Shimmering it sits as they make their way to the water's edge.
Cradled in soft moonlight it glows like the sheen glinting off of silvery knives.

I often steal glances from behind the gossamer veil.
Sometimes a chill down their spines and other times a fleeting reflection in a vast sea.

I tried to show my father what was left of me.
As he stared at the ocean waves, I stood behind him, my fading smile reflected upon the Cerulean.
He turned his head and instantly looked away,
Called it his imagination after a long winter day.
No longer wishing for a glimpse,
Bereft of any residual curiosity, he strayed away.

There is no place left for me, but in the frail embrace of grief.
I am but a reminder imprisoned in faded photographs.
Abandoned between pages of parchment, stained by petals that once graced my empty coffin.
I haunt this tree and this cerulean sea,
A half hearted attempt at a fulfilling afterlife.

It's funny how my father uses charms against my spectral figure.
Feverishly chants the names of gods he only remembers when feeling fear.
Locks his home in the name of safety,
Shrieks when he realises the scratches on his door were left by me.
What he should fear instead are the horrors his absence created.

My mother's words echo in what's become of my ears,
"Don't dream about a man when you can't appeal to a worthy one."
I should have listened.

She dressed me up in the silk dresses and tangerine gowns she stole,
Gossamer veils covered the blue under my eyes.
Pink ribbons were quickly wrapped around the bruises on my wrist.
My dainty little lips were split open from the blows.
Blood often smeared crimson coloured regrets over the words I wished to speak
"Rosy lips, dimple chin. Cover your wounds and smile", she would say.

When she combed my hair I silenced my own groans, let her tear away at the tangles.
Only wincing when she wasn't looking, gazing upon the knots hidden deep beneath my chest.

She would marvel at the shine of the silky white bows in my hair.
Refusing to acknowledge the blood that would be shed after.
Looking away from the splattered patterns it left in my golden braids.

"Now listen up Goldilocks, you find your way into
the right home and you bring back as much as you
can okay?"

So I learnt to smile through the pain.
Learnt to accept the scraps of love I was given.
Wrapping myself in hatred, I tried over and over
again.
I should have known my efforts would be in vain.
Men that reminded me of my mother could never
heal my pain.

It's the Sixteenth today, I know better than to think
you wouldn't come.
And there you are!
My lifeless eyes watch as you stare at the water,
You look so harmless, so serene.
Nothing like the man I know you to be.

The lights flicker and I watch you grimace.
What did you see?
Perhaps glimpses of the secret we share, the one
you hid in this very sea.

I remember smiling up at you.
I remember telling myself we were a fairytale, the
ones my mother forced me to enact.
You carved your anger into my skin and I called it art.

You screamed at my inhibitions and I called it the woes of a difficult lover.
But now I go back to the night you slapped me awake.
My hips pressed against your waist and your knife against my chest.
The bruises you left were traitors,
So you did as is done to the treacherous.

Ashes that once shaped broken women haunt these waves.
Homage to the burdens that haunted my forgotten sisters' days.
Silvery urns left behind by grieving fathers spell out several names.
Lives lost to captors and false claims.

The scars aren't visible anymore.
The blood has been washed away.
My body drowned
My screams muffled.
You left my corpse to rot, shrouded in the teal of these waves.
Slit open my neck and called it an honest mistake.

That's the thing about secrets, they could betray.
Chandeliers shatter and roses decay.
The iron chains you shackle your regrets with rust and eventually give way.

I understand now.
These restless waters remind you of the way I struggled against your will.
It's been Six years now, but you come back here still.
You became a prisoner to your fears,
Afraid of someone finding my rotting corpse here,
Your cerulean stained secret, a mess of bones wrapped in shells and sea nettle.

If only you knew how these vines bind my bones.
Keep them chained the way you once did.
At the bottom of the ocean, these emerald ropes claim.
No one even remembers my name.
No one will know the promises you made.
No one will recognise the woman you betrayed.
The consequences of your disdain are only mine to face.

So on moonlit July evenings like these,
I sit on my beloved Jamun tree.
Hands resting against the bark where my name sits carved,
Looking out at the cerulean waves of the sea.
Staring at the moon, I sing a broken woman's ballad,
One you won't ever have to sing with me.

The Orange Jhoomkas

As I sit perched on my windowsill,
I feel my jhoomkas swaying in the gentle breeze.
Red and yellow blend together in a saffron
synchrony.
The sounds these delicate trinkets make
Remind me of how gentle your voice could be.

Nostalgia creeps in unnoticed on winter evenings
like these.
Everytime I look down at the bruised flesh that
shrouds my hips,
I'm reminded of the taste of your hatred, clashing
against my own.

I remember the mug of chai you would grasp in
your hands,
Your trusted companion on cold nights.
With generous strands of saffron on warm hazel
waves,
Swimming like glowing embers,
Ablaze like the inferno inside my chest.
Encaged within the brittle bars of a cage made of
bones,
The same ones you bruised.

I used to smile and stare into the grey of your eyes,
Melancholy was etched in the depths of your iris.
A storm brewed inside of you,
And you used me as a canvass for the vehemence
you housed inside
With careful measures that were often as brute as
you.

When you weren't carrying mugs in your shivering
hands,
You carried rage.
The kind your father's blows shaped on Autumn
evenings.
The kind that coloured your childhood in blues.
A turquoise that would bruise my skin later,
An ever darkening purple hue.

On the days I did your bidding, did exactly as you
asked
You would pull me in closer, call me your best
girl,
As I would brace myself for when the warmest
hugs would inevitably turn to deadly blows.

I learnt to cover the consequences of your punches
with foundation.
Pink shades of rouge and red shades of eyeshadow
became faithful companions.
Colours helped paint over the pain,

So I would wrap myself in layers of the same hues,
Everyday, all over again.
Alas, it was in vain.

Your grey eyes were home to me, I was your kin.
The family I didn't want but had to accept,
For blood binds and tearing apart those shackles is an unforgivable sin.
You tried to love me, but you failed Baba.
On your last winter night,
I made you a warm cup of chai.
Sprinkled the saffron, and mixed in the poison to set myself free,
Spoonfuls of sugar masked my intent.
I couldn't land blows as fatal as yours, so I gave you a death as sweet as could be.
Abiding by your rules to the very end,
You said my worth lay in what I could make in the kitchen,
So I used my greatest asset.
The irony brought an end to your tyranny.

After I closed your eyelids,
I gripped the shovel and buried your body,
Under my breath I whispered,
"Did I do well, Baba? Did I make you proud?"

Winter evenings now reek of nostalgia,
And all I feel is hatred for the love I still hold for you.

I miss the way your arms held the warmth of
sunshine,
And dread the wreckage they left behind.
Despite it all, I miss the chaos you brought with you.

Why did you teach me to wait outside doors that
were only slammed shut?
To rejoice in the blows that landed square against
my bleeding gut?
Scars I hid behind Amber shawls shrouded my
childhood,
Scars your father inflicted upon your body
shrouded yours.

Even though you're dead,
Peace hasn't crossed my threshold yet.
I slam the door shut, blinded by my dread.

Now as I sit perched on my windowsill,
I feel my jhoomkas sway in the gentle breeze.
Red and Gold blend together, a saffron synchrony.
The sounds these delicate trinkets make,
Remind me of how gentle you could be.
After all you bought me these earrings,
And now they're all that's left of you and the man
you used to be.

The Last Teak Box

Prompt - Think of a memory, your most cherished one. Now picture a world where you are required to abandon the very place you call home. You must prepare to leave the planet you've considered home for the entirety of your life. All you can take with you is a box. It can hold a single memory, and all your other memories will be erased as soon as you depart.

I was ten years old when my mom told me the
world would end in 2012.
So I packed a bag and hid under my bed,
Immortal.
A counter productive decision, adult me thinks.

Hellfire sounds like a made up word.
Just three syllables,
Shrouded within tombs that scriptures crafted.
It couldn't possibly rain down on us tomorrow.
Yet, here I am,
Cradling this teak box.
Combing through the crevices of my brain,
Dragging,
Dredging,
Picking my memories apart.

Who do I run to when I can't remember?
Won't be able to remember,
Will never be allowed to remember.

How do I work with a clean slate,
When all the canvasses I've painted have been left bleeding?
White cloth disguised in shades of crimson,
An angry hue, a vengeful cry.
All my art speaks of is melancholy.

Who will I be if the only memory I keep isn't filled with grief?

How do I walk up to the ocean and gift her my memories,
When I once promised her my ashes.
When I turn to dust,
Will I not return to dust?

If I have to make a choice,
I'll take you, if not as a whole, then as a memory.
A scrap, a remnant,
A single line from the story you wrote with me.

I have to wake up tomorrow and accept your absence,

Welcome an ending,
Dress it up as a fresh start.
But the glass isn't half full when you're not here to hold it.

I wish I could take with me the perfume on your neck,
Filling the air I breathe on Sunday evenings.
The jokes you've made about church every Thursday
Are etched in my brain and the unholy words I recite are yours to keep.
You've painted my Friday's green with the hues of your printed shirts
How do I carry with me what's forced to perish?
All the way
To a place so far away from home, it reminds me of my mother.

My choice has been taken away from me,
That's not new territory,
Never has been.
I'm used to condescension and I'm used to loss.
Grief doesn't scare me,
Though I wish it would sink into the ocean,
Sink with the ashes I've held in my hands.

When we land upon the blue sands of an alien nation,
They'll brand it a new beginning.
But the glass will be half empty when your hands aren't holding it.

So in my box I shall keep the memory of our first hug.
It's coloured by the wings of butterflies,
The same ones that sat within my stomach,
As I waited for a chance to see you for the first time,
Beyond a screen.
Beyond those sentences you carefully crafted
For the unforgiving audience that a dating app houses.
But there you were, adorned in black,
Cradling a bouquet of carnations.

I felt the warmth of your smile and the safety of your touch
When you hugged me and said my name out loud,
I wanted to belong to you and never part ways.

I hoped to not have to count my cents and save my dimes.
To get into unknown cars,
Leading to rooms where your eyes are on mine.

To not have to spend another 100 phone calls,
Wishing, praying, hoping for your voice,
Right next to mine.
Chalking out the days of the week,
On the most colour coded calendar in the world.
I only want to step foot on new ground
If the very next second turns into a reminder of what you mean to me.
I'll scour the metallic waters and the turquoise sands,
In search of your hands.

And as the salt air burns my lungs,
I know I will not remember you tomorrow.
But I would die at the feet of a God I don't believe in,
For a chance to love you again.

When I enter a world without my selfhood, bereft of love,
All I ask from this fragile fragment of memory,
Is that it colours me whole and forces me into action.
I demand that it pushes, shoves and reminds me to look for you.
Holds me by the neck and forces me to urgency's door.

Because without you,
I'll become a coffin buried underground before its time.
Covered in the brown of rot, obscured by the absence of light.
I demand that my love for you is awoken from its dormancy.

I demand you,
All over again.

The Crystals I Bathe in Moonlight

When I was a little girl,
I would dream of finding true and pure love,
On snowy hills and morbid mountains,
Where I was told fairytales took birth.

When I was a little girl,
I would dream of finding a prince seated on my window sill,
Dressed in a beautiful satin gown,
As white as the snow and as warm as an amber fire.
Breathing against the stained glass,
His lipstick intact, yet gently smeared on his gleaming, broken teeth.

When I was a little girl,
I would dream of finding love
And every day I swore, to gently kiss him under the mistletoe,
Hold his hands,
Stop the snow from taking away the warmth he so desperately deserved.

His icy blue veins pressed up against my auburn waves,
The snow beneath us would crumble.
Eventually giving way to dark desires and warm blue sunshine,
Almost as impure as the horrors that lurk within.

I would make him mittens and ugly jumpers,
Hot cocoa as warm as burning embers floating on lava,
The type that could stop his heart from beating, and revive the dead that haunted his dreams.

Occasionally, I would use my delicate crystal sword, to protect him from his past and the monsters that made his beautiful mind their refuge.

I would be his princess in shining armour,
Riding in on a sleigh; served by Blue eyed and Ivory furred wolves.
Travelling through decades of snow covered tombstones,
With a burning ferocity;
Sunflower yellow teeth bared,
Intensity that could make the frigid, immovable crystals crumble,
Just as easily as my dreams had.

The papery white flakes, resting gently against my scattered Orange freckles,
Falling reluctantly onto my frozen lips.

I promise I would save him in a heartbeat.
Fall in love with his ocean blue eyes,
Happily drowning in the feelings that bubbled up inside the pit of my stomach.
Every time he bites his bleeding sapphire lips.
I carefully lap up the remnants of his shunned and broken rubies
Use his pulse to keep my caged heart from stopping.

I would make him feel loved in the simplest of ways.
Be his princess in my shining Golden armour,
Hair adorned with dew drops and gold leaves;
Midas would wage war against my radiance;

I would be the love of his life.

Waking up every morning,
Just to make him warm pancakes,
Delicately topped with fluff as soft and delicate as his flaming auburn hair.
Maple syrup as smooth as sunshine.
I wanted to place cherries on his sundaes, just so I could bite them off when he wasn't looking.

Impatiently waiting for him to steal my crystal cherry,
so I could watch it break and shatter like brittle glass between his Ruby lips.
Gently wiping the blood away with my azure silk napkin.
Suddenly everything was as purple as my satin sheets.
The ones that lay patient, waiting for us under the forsaken pillow fort.
The One I built with my scarred scabby hands,
The home where nightmares go to die.

The Crystals I Bury in Moonlight

The only love I had ever known,
Was found in dark alleys and bankrupt brothels.
Romance meant for cheap table cloths and breakable cutlery,
Drops of wine served to the emaciated in dusty chalices;
The occasional condom, lying peacefully, undisturbed and unwanted inside a cracked glass dome.

Sex was never an option, it was always a livelihood.

It had been imprinted onto our very souls,
In the form of scars that reek of cheap liquor and flashy golden bracelets,
Buried in a rich man's yellowing tooth.
Fairy tales where there were poisoned apples, cracked mirrors, burning spirits and alcohol that could set fire to your iridescent soul.

Bedtime stories where giant metal poles impaled fragile emerald butterflies,
Leaving behind nothing but a mystic crystalline void.

The occasional cracked Scarlet lipstick placed on a
decaying Oakwood dresser.
French windows that let in a waning moon,
weeping blood sapphire tears,
Washed up mermaids stuck in lifeless oceans,
Gentle moonlight that drips on broken tiaras
And priceless wine spilt carelessly on loose
floorboards,
locked away in underground cellars.

A house made of frosted beach glass,
Firmly buried under grains made of pearls.
The helpless cries of dead prisoners,
echoing in the graveyards that surrounded us.

We didn't know what it was like to be cherished
and held affectionately by a sunless sea,
Not having to hope for a better future,
As we cried tears of blood and lust,
Screamed to the deaf and wildly gestured to the
blind.

We were sold by the dozen and starved to make
sure we didn't use up too much bronzer,
After all, there was only one container, and
fourteen of us had frostbitten, swollen fingers.
Broken cheekbones don't need concealing under
decades of bruise and grime

Our secrets were laid out on the table and covered
in stained washcloth,
a shrine,
as dry and thin as the raw skin that resides
between my thighs,
used and abused,
Black and Blue,
Red and Gold,
Pink and Purple,
A gorgeous rainbow in a sky that has been painted
in despair.

A spectrum,
So endless
Yet buried and forgotten,
By the very ancestors that birthed it, in a broken
down hospital.

Lime green tiles in a pitch black corridor,
Mahogany wood ceilings that constantly reek of
death.
The stench that comes with unwanted pregnancies,
crimson rivulets flowing down scarred skin,
shrivelled toenails, loose strands of hair, breaking
waters, lonely sobs, stale blood, dried mothballs
stuck in the skeletons of one's past, greying soap,
relentless skid marks, desperate scribbles, torn
cloth, broken earrings and funeral pyres.

I had snakes for pets and bitches in prison,
Switchblades up my sleeves and army knives in my pockets.

Fireplaces were funeral pyres,
The home where nightmares are birthed, and children are laid to rest.

The Glass House

I find myself waking up each day, trapped in a glass house
Sometimes, it's a window to the utopia that exists outside
Sometimes, just a broken mirror

Rotting vines surround me
Faded bougainvilleas form a beautiful wreath that I cannot seem to tear through

I wake up clothed in soiled and gauzy night suits,
Sometimes it's ice cold tears that leave blazing trails down my chest, sometimes it's the metallic tang of blood.
I can't stop chewing on my torn nails
Using their broken fragments to gnaw at my war worn heart
It refuses the cage I throw at it
Why can't I stop crying?
On moonlit nights, blood and grime intermingled with the pain of isolation, is all I taste

My heart keeps pounding against these grimy
windowpanes, refusing to give up
"Foolish!" I scream
After all, refusing to shy away from the impossible
is a devastating habit
She knows the glass will always refuse to shatter

I beg my own reflection, but she looks back at me,
equally helpless

Yet, she keeps trying
Screaming and begging
But the gatekeeper who holds the keys, keeps his
eyes wide open, unblinking, staring, chuckling
mirthlessly at my helplessness.
He smiles down at me and ever so slightly shakes
his beautiful head

Refusing to acknowledge the shadows that
reek indefinitely of unending despair, is also a
devastating habit

I wonder how many more cuts I'll need to inflict
on myself, just to invite his humanity into this
devastatingly beautiful room
How many more illusions will I have to brave,
before I accept the reality that keeps me enclosed?

His hollow chest beats with a resigned sense of disgust
I look for his heart but all I find is the never ending void that would engulf my existence if I chose to shatter these walls
That's where the wind chimes reside
I hear them now

Ever so occasionally, he pokes at the glass
Without a second's pause, a shard effortlessly moves and gives way to the chill that resides only in coffins shrouded with grief

I see the moon
I wonder why she weeps

Gleaming tear soaked crystals, gently dancing in the wind
Falling ever so softly in waves that refuse to engulf me

I stare as the tiny crystals shatter
Why can't I be granted the same mercy?
Which temple do I crawl to?
Do they even allow the faithless anymore

I can hear the wind chimes again, or are those the screams of the forsaken?
I can't tell anymore.

Funny how sunlight often creates rainbows that
burn through your skin, leaving behind nothing but
regrets and irreplaceable scars

I rush to the craters he so nonchalantly creates
I'm on my hands and knees again
I can feel the footprints I left behind
A time when blind hope and delusional curiosity
dared to exist within the factions of my brokenness
My weather worn heart has been shattered, but the
foolish child refuses to stop weeping
I look up at him, tears brimming in my eyes,
refusing to fall
Alas! The cuts on my cheek can't take more despair

"Let me out, hold my hand, please save me"

He refuses to budge, just stares with his dark
brown orbs
They radiate a kindness that isn't available to me
Warmth, I will never be privy to
I feel the cold drought slicing through my rib cage
Is this why the moon weeps?

"Rip my heart out"
I beg
But nobody's listening
The moon stares down at me, a romanticised
reflection of the devastation I cage inside

"Save me" I whisper
"Only you can" she whispers back
We both tremble under the indifferent galaxies that stretch out above us
Gentle ripples in the moonlight remind me of the decaying Pearls I left behind in the graveyards that reek of grief

I gnaw and I scratch with, and at what's left of my soul
Screaming to be let out of this gleaming utopia
Here, the reflection of my bloodied and battered smile, haunts me

I see right through the facade as the crowd gathers around
Rosy lips soaked with blood, bruised cheeks that cage a battered, yet dimpled chin
Gentle love bites, a careless lover disguises as a warm caress
They all tell stories that nobody wishes to listen to
But the dead gather anyway
Hungry for anything that tastes like familiarity

My desperation doesn't seem to leave this decadent enclosure
The people stare unabashed
Pointing and smiling as I dance with my war worn heart

The guard's piercing eyes seem to shine with the power he holds over me
I'm trapped by my own inability to break through these walls
They stand fragile, yet taunting, much like the time he yanked my hair and forced himself into my broken and battered rib cage
Why won't she stop beating? I have no blood left to give to these grimy floors

As I twirl, I feel what's left of my arms reach out for a stray shard

I finally hear her stop
Relief is what engulfs me instead of his arms
The tireless beat no longer needs itself heard
And as the perfect crystal is embedded in my throat
The blood now flows in tiny unstoppable rivulets on the grimy tear stained floor
Making its way out through the bullet holes this house was built on
Shattering the very nightmare, I called existence

The crowd erupts into tumultuous applause
I hear the door hinges creak
Here she comes

Another victim
Completely blinded by the beauty of a woman that can't refuse,
Enchanted by the light and its twinkling dances.

Well, as they say, the show must go on
Even on this despicable and forgotten moor

Are those wind chimes I hear?

As I sit on my bougainvillea tree, singing my siren song
All the audience hears, is the occasional wind chime

So they hurriedly look away from the petal strewn graveyards
Terrified of who, or what they may find
A broken lover
Or perhaps his embrace

Why don't you come down to the glass house?
Where the light dances with the ones it's caged

We have flowers, mirrors and women with gentle hearts, perfect for every broken man's rage

The Castle of the Dead

I sit on this secluded marble throne
It's as cold as the loneliness I surround myself with
Staring out at the frozen rivers that house the dead
Through these frosted sapphire windows
I gently beckon to them
"Rise."

Bring me the diamonds that surround your coffins
and adorn your broken necks
I need them to tear at my war worn heart
She only lets the most decadent destroy
And when I'm done, I shall wear them around
what's left of my hands
Ruby red, and carefully drenched in the blood of a
scorned woman
Shining brighter than the embers that have
shaped me

I'm screaming, hoping against hope that the
destruction I house inside, will finally free itself.

I wonder
If I scream loud enough, will his fingerprints free
themselves, off of my chest

And away from my lifeless body?
Don't dress me up in frocks this time
I'm told that pretty bows and frills, only attract the vile

You can't hear me through these walls made of glowing embers
They manage to burn through the facades I create
Every time I stand up with the blue fire that burns inside of the hollow I call a chest,
I wake up with bruises as dark as the midnight sky, and as tragic as the blues the oceans hold prisoner

Reducing me to nothing, but sparks that fade out
Leaving behind nothing but abandoned wood fires

I think you can hear me, but you choose to pretend its the storm that's wailing
After all, what sane man wishes to be haunted by the screams of his fading lover
I lurk behind your rosewood cabinets on moonlit nights
Kiss your neck when you aren't watching
Smile at your children and steal glances at your wives,
Hide myself in the attic
Occasionally finding the courage to look up at the photos that house the smile I lost

Funny how your disdain seeps into every crevice
you forget to fill with pretence
Flinching when your children are around
I wonder why you look away when they look up at
you
Could it be the burnt Auburn hair, that stinks of
rotting flesh? Gently swaying in the Autumn wind
Green eyes that glow in the dark, terrorising even
the skeletons you keep caged in your closet
Fangs that cut sharper than broken emeralds,
gleaming like the churches you've shunned
Claws that reside in nightmares, that only the dying
dare to haunt

Are you scared of the dead my love?
Oh don't be, we care the most.

I begged for you to love me
I ached for you to hold me with your broken hands
But your Midas touch turned my heart into
something that shimmers but never truly shines
They store gold in pretty little cabinets, I wish you
did too,
I would wear it around my neck and call myself a
princess,
Shunned queens belong in coffins and shunned
women belong in walls.
You taught me that, dear lover.

They say, "All that glitters is not gold."
They should know, all that's buried is not dead

I stare at the floors you've stored my ashes in
As I smell the smoke that comes with inevitable decay
I find myself bleeding from crevices that will never know light

This is why I sit by the dead on lonely evenings
Begging to be included
Bang my bruising fists against these rusting tombstones
Pleading for an answer

But what do the dead know?
Apart from the grief of lost love and secrets no one bothered to unearth

Your sapphire eyes are blinded by tears
And my torn skin is jagged from torture that lasts beyond its years
The grief I shroud myself with?
You've always called it lunacy

I wonder if anyone hears me howling behind these blood curling giggles
Funny how blood curls when it doesn't even exist

Perhaps the mist I use to hind behind abandoned walls will show me mercy?
After all, blood knows no language, except the ones bred in war,
At the womb of destruction and the halls of mortal fear,
It demands to be shed,
And shed I shall.

The Blind Mother

If you steal from a jar of olives, are you then a thief
or were you hungry?
If I take a piece of the bread on your plate, am I
exhibiting savagery or are you just too brute to
share?
I'll carve up sticks of butter, would you then call it a
crime?
Why must the world devour, when the brute
hunger is mine?

In a world where we know darkness prevails,
Why must morality be a sword, one that karma
wields?
With hatred burning her hair to ashes, her dress
aflame,
Why must we call upon her with the dulcet tones of
revenge?
Reducing her to her anger,
Is there nothing more we see

Are we blind to her anguish, blind to her pain?
Is karma not a woman?
Has she never felt the shudder of her breasts
Or the pain and blood of motherhood?

Does she not remember the rawness of a
newborn's bite, the touch of an elder, a lonely
sunless night?
The smell of burning bridges and the sight of
abandoned cribs,
Didn't they once make her eyes ache?
Does she not remember the burden of carrying a
womb?
The woman that birthed morality,
The son that turned around and spat on her chest.

Does she not know the pain of humanity?
Is justice not a blindfolded wench?
Has she not felt the vulnerability of darkness,
The silk cloth it's bound with.
Holding scales in her hands, walking into gallows,
Has she never been burnt by the weight of
judgement?
Felt the anguish of a life lost to stones on a
balancing bridge

Does she not breathe in the hatred
The smoke in the air,
Must make her lungs hurt too,
All her daughter's do.
Has she not had her vows stolen? Thrown upon her
wake?

Left alone at the altar?
A crying heaving mess.
Is that not who karma is?

A woman.

It was a man after all that betrayed the First god and now it's a woman who holds him in her arms,
Tearing off her breasts to meet his needs, suckle the calf and pacify his cries,
I wonder why the kingdom of heaven is quite tonight,
With gods hiding behind locked doors and angels with broken wings,
There are shiny halos all over the floor,
Where is the justice in all of this?

My father told me I was a curse that befell him one night
Told me I was made of darkness,
I see him wishing upon shooting stars every night,
Crying out loud for blinds that keep the dead out, or perhaps to be blinded by the seeping void,
I drip my mercurial sadness as I go,
I wonder why the kingdom of heaven is quite tonight.

But I was made of sorrow and I turned it blue,
Now I have these nightingales trapped in my ribcage,
They cry every night but its not songs of pain,
Not anymore,
My father's wishes did come true.
Now he wishes for sunsets and rainbows, and all he ever gets are wells and moats,
Ask and ye shall receive,
But the kingdom of heaven is quite tonight.
So he doesn't look at the boats that are burning on the ghats,
An inferno resting on tranquility.
The kingdom of heaven has fallen,
Does that mean we do too?

He makes me want to hide myself behind cupboards,
Stealing glances at him and fixing my hair,
Painting on a tight smile, one even the world's most faded washcloth cannot remove,
But I'll defend him still, wielding my sword,
Putting on a blindfold as thick as my pain,
Holding onto my beliefs for dear life,
Because darkness isn't palatable to everyone.

But she exists in the night, hiding behind her mother who is now the moon,
And the women that have become stars,

Buried in graves of ivory and ivy,
They smile down at passing cries.
Karma must be down there they think,
Wielding her sword yet again.

But she's just the woman at our doorstep,
The angel with no wings,
She lives in the breaths we take and the pain we feel,
Crouching behind thresholds and fireplaces of marble,
Slowly sinking in.
She's breaking through the cracks now,
She's left her sword behind.

Karma is a woman, not the one we believe,
She doesn't wish to shed blood, or watch her daughters weep.
Crawling through fireplaces, because she's never invited,
But when she sits comfortably by a warm mantle piece,
Decorated with the smiles of multiple Christmases, grief amiss
She sees the family picnics and remembers the smell of warm bread,
Gingerbread cookies in the oven,
Children resting in their cribs.

She is not blind to suffering, only waiting to ease it,
A seemingly heartless entity, with a heart as
loud as the roaring fire you house beneath your
mantelpiece.
A mother with a gauzy blindfold, one she never
put on.
Oh, but it's off now.

"Invite the pain in" she says,
"Invite me in, after all I am your mother",
She will bathe you in moonlight and replace your
Scarlet lullabies,
Your bedroom ceiling will be painted Azure tonight
As she lulls you to sleep, you'll see
Morality is nothing but a sharp picture,
Like the one with Oranges next to your window,
Covered in the colours we build binaries with.

Morality is a hard scale on the back of your hand
and karma is the one that heals,
A soft touch, a teacher, once a lover, once a stranger
But today, a mother and a wife.
Married to the love she understands.

You don't have to tell her,
She knows what moonlight means to you,
It's her songs you've been yearning for,
You can hold her close to you.

The conversations you'll share tonight,
Hold them close like you would a father's embrace,
She knows what it means to love you, she isn't here to hurt
Only to hold the child she's been yearning for,
Invite her in, won't you?

The Mirror That Spoke of Tombstones

I kneel in front of this forsaken mirror,
The wise one, gifted with the gaze of truth.
The very one my mother presented to me,
As a form of discipline, of course.

Remember your worth, she said,
Smiling as she broke my bones and scratched my rib cage open,
Ever so gently,
With the words she often spoke.
She struck with unhealed hands,
Still covered in bruises her birth-giver once inflicted.
A trail of devastation and battered young women,
Is all this circle has birthed.
A path littered with tombstones,
Names etched with blood.
Night falls and the cycle devours,
An unstoppable, immovable rut.

Tired past my years,
Grieving just out of reach of the world's ears,
The dungeon lights flicker,
And with them my belief.

What keeps me alive still?
All that remains are these shackles.
Roses form shrouds over the grime of these silver necklaces.
They etch out a story of potential,
Forever curbed,
Forever chained,
Endlessly restrained.

Cover your destruction with roses,
And the world will be quick to call it a funeral.
Suddenly you're surrounded by mourners.
Every last one grieving,
For the woman you should have been.

But noone peers into the Rose covered caskets,
Blinded by their Rose tinted glasses,
Refusing to witness the mundane monstrosity, the infirm once lived to be.
They hide behind their lace threaded gloves,
Lifting their powdered arms,
Shedding one tear after another,
Over the woman you could have been.

Carefully dressing you up in the insecurities they inherited,
Disguised as Scarlet bows,
They coil around the curls of your hair,
And now that your soul has been shrouded in the name of tradition,
You're a prisoner, worse for wear.

They cage you in dilapidated dungeons and throw away the key,
Call tired women the epitome of beauty.
Reduce her to nothing, but the dances she performs,
So very gracefully.
Clad like a ballerina in her iron shackles,
Do you feel her pulsating agony?

When I stare at the fragments of this mirror,
A deserted loveless dungeon,
An illusion built with finesse.
I see flashes of the violence,
That was once mine to keep.

In silken gift wrapped packages,
The size of cages I've put my dreams in.
The size of bruises lining my calves.
Hidden in plain sight,
Much like the woman I desired to be.

Men that wouldn't love me,
Mothers that wouldn't dare,
Fathers that refused to,
And boys that shouldn't care,
Cut my heart open with switch-knives they named cruelty.
As cold as the cobblestone my feet bleed upon,
Even icicles would have shown mercy.

As you lift up my satin gown,
Staring with wonder at the scars you see,
Growing ever so incessantly on me,
Do you know their stories?
How they've bled through sunsets,
And the bouquets of Violets, rage herself presents?
They've coloured my rib cage like a faded painting,
Outside, on a warm summer day.
A kaleidoscope of grief,
Coloured in as a present, to the woman I could not be.

Why must I hide away the Greens of jealousy that color my skin?
Turn it a feverish red,
Persuasive in their charms,
There's no escaping those Emerald arms.
Bend my head in shame around other women,

Stab myself in the neck and call it a service?
Why must I hack away at pieces of myself and then call it art?

What is the benefit of greater good if it only brings greater betrayal?
Why must I bandage my lover's scars everytime he drives dagger shaped words into mine?
Why must I smile, when he scoffs and traces the curves of my fears?
Teasing them with every sentence, each word a new wound.
Deeper, and deeper, till there's nothing left.
Slowly, I'm on my way,
To the woman he's making me.

Why must I stab at the little girl that cowers within me?
Why must I hurt her to please the rainbows of cruelty that encircle me?
They come in the shapes of war worn people,
And name my destruction love,
Teaching me to caress these wounds with never ending patience,
When will it be enough?

Why must I slap this child and pick away at her scars?
Why must I set alight her fragile hopes,

With matches lit by a man's desire?
Flames that burn the Browns of her hopeful eyes,
destroying the pinks of her smile.
The same smile that once believed in fairytales and magical balls,
The land of the fae,
Where music builds glass castles, and night never falls.

Why must I tear away at the roses she uses to pay homage to herself?
Why must I drive daggers into her brittle glass irises?
Stealing away her dreams like a common thief in a man's world.

Shouldn't I be stealing away glass slippers from unworthy princes,
Placing them on her dainty little feet instead?
Watching her shatter transparent ceilings, breaking chandeliers in her wake.

The bloodshed from the world's wars, seeps into my chest.
It finds a way to my shrunken heart.
I refuse to flinch against the Scarlet scent of defeat.
So I bend down, and cover up these Peonies,
Painting over them with the silver of my tears,

The amber of my pain,
And the lilac of my grief.
Painting a picture around the bruises that shape me,
A phoenix with broken wings.
Covering my rib cage with blankets of rotting Lilies,
Broken kaleidoscopes of grief,
A present to the girl I once wished to be.

Shards of glass build a castle within me,
The world wishes I would hide it,
Destruct it,
Let it burn.

But I ask yet again,
Why must I feel the Emerald shades of shame?
Why must I hack away at my breasts?
Ensuring they fit, nice and snug,
Unsafe in the hands of my unhappy lover.

Why must I put on rose tinted shades that blind those around me?
Why must I stare at broken silver mirrors,
Grimacing at the flaws I've called mistakes?
Why must I save fragments that the moonlight brings me,
Only cut away at my own will?

Why must I carve a smile onto my scarred face and giggle?
Careful not to be heard, never to be seen.
I cackle at the audacity of men and their bare ballads.
Hiding us behind gauzy curtains and glass slippers?
What happens when the veil shifts?

Why must I carry the burden of a broken mother's rage?
Why must I hate the very vessel that holds me?
The very casket that holds my burnt soul.
The very urn that cradles the ashes of my dreams.
My body is now a burial ground with stories to tell,
The childhood I burnt with flames of disgust and hatred,
The little girl I chased into a pit littered with Tangerine snakes.

I could hear her screams as the butterflies around her were branded,
With forked tongues and venomous words,
Slowly retreating into their cocoons.
Shedding their silk wings to fit gossamer ones.
This was the price of unquestionable beauty.
A virtue that is a lie,
For she can never be attained, only desired.
Like a moth to an everlasting flame.

A flame littered with the Blues of Peonies,
Resting atop a grave.
The one that's been reserved,
For the woman I wasn't allowed to be.

A flame devouring the Saffron of abandoned dreams.
Burning away brightly on funeral pyres.
Homages built with rotting wood,
From the magical woods that shroud desires.
The very woods that have now been decapitated,
To build these burning homes for the dead.

In the end,
All we have is another graveyard,
Littered with the lives of women that should have lived.

Try and look for what makes me happy and you'll find yourself lost,
Much like the woman I turned out to be.

Bury me with my dreams.
This urn has a billion patterns etched on her.
None I'd like to see.
But bury me by the seaside,
Let the waves wash over me.
Perhaps the Azure of the oceans will remind me,
Of the little girl I once used to be.

I still try, as I lie in my grave,
Still trying to be,
Who she wished to see,
Everytime she looked at a Crimson mirror, as
broken as a gravestone can be.

A Half Written Legacy – Part I

Smoke travels past our windows,
The fog has finally emerged.
Thick and unforgiving,
She's out for blood.
No longer contained within the recesses of my mind,
She's exactly what I'd imagined she'd be.

It's here now,
The dreaded hour of death.
It's been minutes,
But I never heard the clock tick, and there isn't a deafening gong in these woods.
There are no angels with wings, and no monsters with scales,
It's just me and these woods, up in fumes and flames.
The train, high and mighty, deafening in its roar, is now a fallen soldier.
Engulfed by the light,
Drowning in it,
Devoured, consumed.

The woods look like they're burning too,
A bonfire perhaps,
For the heavens above to celebrate with.
Everything happens for a reason, and maybe this is what the god's needed,
A break,
An inferno,
A final burning.

Maybe the falling snow, is just bits of celestial marshmallow,
Roasted over the screams of many last breaths,
Or maybe it's just dust.
My mother did always say I had an over active imagination,
But I can't tell if it's the debris or the ashes in the dim moonlight.

Could one burnt cigarette, really bring about Judgement day?
An inferno for a Hundred souls?
One stone and a Million birds,
All fleeing into the night,
One cold body dropping mute after the other.

Is Judgement day just another moment then?
A fleeting second that has now become, the rest of our infernal lives?
On an abandoned train,

A shaking vestibule,
A carriage that was meant to lead the way.
Take you to your next second,
And somehow it brought us to our last.

When do you know it's time to start cherishing?
When do you know it's time to be grateful?
For your last rendezvous,
Slipping carelessly into a Cherry red booth,
milkshakes and ice freezes in hand.
Do you notice the stench of winter dripping down the sides of your cup?
Could ice ever be so unrelenting with its warmth?
Do omens really come disguised?

Do you realise you're One step away from the silence that's waiting by the door?
Glassy eyed, ravenous, eager to consume, all that you took for granted.
The music you played on the radio every Saturday, on your way to school.
The casually scribbled lyrics on your wall.
The ringtones that you detest and your little Blue alarm.
The way your friend's voice lights up with every note of a giggle,
And the wind chimes by your doors,
Sleeping.
Lulled to silence,

A graveyard of broken bones and jarring musical notes.
Now they'll play this silent song at your funeral,
And a new ballad shall be born.

Do you take a step back when you see black cats passing by, chant furiously in your mind?
Or do you shake it off as just another silly superstition,
Laughing, hands intertwined,
One step away from your final hug goodbye.

What happened to the multiple wishes I made, standing patiently by frosted birthday cakes?
The affirmations under my pillow and the candles I blew out.
A thousand dandelions reduced to golden specks in the wind,
Now just dust, floating by.
A couple million prayer books,
All burnt to the bone.
The skeletal remains of the force, we so lovingly called Hope.

Sharing meals on pearl laden plates with your chosen family,
Warm lights and ruby red chalices lit up by our smiles,
Never afraid of the pearls coming undone,

Because when they would, and they inevitably did,
We'd string together new ones.
The never ending cycle of life.

But what happens when the circle maker snatches
the pearls that string together your smile?
A picture replaces the warmth of your breath and
the gleam in your eyes,
And suddenly, your cage is an alter disguised as a
coffin.
There's people shedding tears and eulogies
afloat,
But your pink dress is buried in the garden,
And no one remembers the perfume you wore.

Where is the swing set we bought when I was
Eighteen?
Where does it lay now?
Behind the garden shed, or beside my lost bicycles?
What colour was it again?
I realise I forgot.
On my way to yet another morning,
Spent dreaming about how I would live out the rest
of my days.
Home was a fantasyland, safe within the depths of
my mind.
Made of the deepest desires that I once governed,
And I am still a princess, but my kingdom is a
funeral pyre.

All the letters I wrote, the chances I abandoned and
the people I scorned,
Do they go up in flames too?
Are we all just fireflies on the path to a burning pit?
Are the gods laughing at my jokes and the words
I've left behind?
Chuckling over my metaphors and shedding ichor
over my lines?
Sighing over the promises that were never mine to
complete,
Do they weep?
Or have my books been tucked away in libraries,
rotting behind empty chairs,
Waiting to be picked up.
Caged within their cyclical grave,
By the force we so lovingly call Time.

My teddybear bed spread lies wrapped up in my
cupboard,
A secret that's no longer mine to keep.
My calendar is lavender, and my candles pink,
But it doesn't matter what shade my collarbones
were,
Because my tombstone reeks of Grey.
The colour that paints over night and calls upon
storms,
Wrapping up the last of the light.
I am the lullaby in the storm,
A legacy that was written as a fairytale,

A warning for the kids, disguised as a graveyard of musical notes.
You'll find me in the touch of a mother's hand,
And in the truces that end conflict in bedrooms on cold June nights.

Why wasn't I told that a random Saturday, was my last chance to put on my Amber dress?
Cover it up in bows and stitch up all the holes.
Why wasn't I told that a random Tuesday, would be my last chance to taste cake?
Lick the frosting right off the top,
Leave a cherry behind, remorseless.
Why didn't I know that yesterday was the last time my mom would have her hands on her hips,
Angrily muttering, because I packed too heavy,
And now there wouldn't be enough space on the godforsaken train.
"It's supposed to be a fun journey!" she had exclaimed.
And it turned out to be, the last one I would ever take.

A Half Hearted Legacy – Part II

I left this carriage,
Three hours ago,
But my body lies here still.
It was a drink of water,
A harmless one.
A few steps to the cooler, and back home to my mother's arms,
But then the world went up in fire, and my feeble cup of water wasn't enough to fan the flames.

Oh well, at least I died trying.

There's dust all around
It's coated all the people at rest,
Like a shroud stitched with the fragments of fate.
Like fine print on the corners of our tickets,
It's consumed the faces we once identified with.

There's flames all around,
And the light looks like rain,
Like early snowfall that somehow arrived late.
Debris found It's home in the air,
It's fine dust and starshine, glinting delicately in the moonlight.

A pretty picture that's painted with a scathing
story in mind.
What does my body have to say when I look over at
her?
Crushed between the weights of wheels that
should never have moved.
The price of fate comes heavy, and it crushes the
pearly white of your bones.

This godforsaken journey has betrayed us all,
But who do the dead lament to?
No paper will register the ink of loss,
It's as fleeting as a memory,
An invisible child of the night.

Maybe as the angels shed tears,
There are stars being added to the sky.
A never ending canvas coloured with shiny streaks
of plight.

But the smell of burnt flesh rotting on these seats
has wiped away all hope,
And now there's people running around screaming,
Families on the floor.
This house of cards has fallen,
A collective final breath drawn.
The air smells of decay,
It never was meant to be dawn.

Here are her pet snakes feasting on my eyes,
The Earth can be a ruthless mother,
Draining my veins for all they've ever held and all they've ever known.
I've never imagined death to be so brutal.
A picture painted with the Emeralds of the relentless mother,
With the blues of my nerves,
With the crimson of my tears and the lavender of my years.
Colours so bright they blind you and leave you gasping for air,
This is the picture that death paints, lonely lovers beware.

This is my attempt at a letter,
At a sign,
The one that the living keep pleading for.
This is me staring out the crushed glass,
Waving the remnants of what used to be, a hand.
I'm screaming at you, begging you to walk away,
Live, while you still can.

A wave to the ones that are alive,
But house death in their eyes.
Crevices filled with dread make homes in the hollows of their bones.

They walk around carrying grief like it's the very child they've birthed,
When really she's a gift, a present from the ones they loved most.
I hurt just from staring at it, but the glass can only cut at my limbs,
They were weak anyway,
A pound of flesh so easily relinquished,
Wrapped up and stitched back together,
Deep in the ground, in the realm where my coffin sits.

I hope they paint with the Cherry Red of my years and the Maroon of my tears.

Dress me up in Beige and say you'll never forget me,
Then drink your sweet tea and dip your roses in water.
I'm just the coffee stains on the tablecloth, and the ink blotches on paper.
I'm as fickle as the rings you keep in your heart shaped lockbox
The one you now use for candles that will never be lit.
I'm all but a prayer on the lips of the damned,
A lullaby in the storm.

I am the chances I never took and the doors I couldn't open,
The man I turned on myself for and the man that never looked back.
I'm the unreturned messages and the unspoken words,
I'm your undoing and I'm the undone.

I live in your memories and rest, buried there too.
I'm the books I read and the books I forgot,
I'm the trips I took and the roads I didn't walk.

I'm in the lines of your palms and the colours lingering on your fingers,
(from that night we sat down with paints.)
I'm the soil that coats the disguised hallows you walk on,
And I'm the mud underneath your forgotten plants.
The orchards you walk by,
I'm the lady in white,
A child of the night.

I am the girls you've loved and the women you've wept with.
I'm in the shadows of the light,
And I reside within the satin curtains that keep out the darkness of the night.
I'm in the silver chalices and in the plastic cups,

I'm hiding behind doorways and haunting your windows.
I'm with you, and I'm without you.

Do you see me? Or am I just a trick of the light,
A flicker in the night,
A figment,
A shadow,
A streak in a lone picture.
Do you see me?
Mom?
Dad?
Hel-

Do you see me?
I'm here and I'm not,
I'm loved but a thing of fear,
I came to you and you wept because you miss me,
But I'm still stuck here.
Haunting your doorways and reliving our memories.

I'm here, do you see me?

Whose gonna read my poems now?
It doesn't matter, cause these words and a feeble wave are all I have, and all I'll rest with.
Even on my tombstone they'll find a place.

They'll squeeze themselves between apostrophes
and broken periods,
They'll find a way.
I'll find a way.
We both,
Always do.
You'll read my half hearted legacy eventually, and
you'll wish there is never one written for you.

She Tastes of Lemons

I walk into grocery stores just to stare at piles of lemons,
And the Ochre they paint themselves with.
A shade so bright it's not easy on the eyes.
How do you turn to your mother and tell her that
Someday you aspire to be as brave as a lemon.
One that's rotting away behind grocery store aisles,
Hidden,
Out of plain sight
Away from the man that touches you, and brands it love.

I wish to stand tall in rooms painted with pallets that wouldn't dare to show themselves.
No one gravitates towards piles and piles of cabbages,
Or the comfort that Earthy Greens believe they hold.
We all recognise the shades of muddy waters as homes we were handed,
And maybe thats why none of us want to reside close,
Close to what's familiar or remotely comforting.

Homes aren't beautiful,
They're broken and constantly rebuilt,
They're dressed in shabby curtains and wooden lamps,
They smell like cold porridge served over unending arguments and torn tablecloths.
Earthy browns make me want to claw at my skin for a hint of crimson,
I never want to feel at home again.

I'd much rather stand beneath the amber glow of street lights,
watching Blue butterflies pass me by.
I'm learning to build a home,
That doesn't teach me to bury my grief in the soft browns of the earth,
But teaches me to frame my resentment against the backdrop of a filthy Orange.
One that highlights all the pain you've been trying to cut out,
From within the cages you've built inside your chest.

I want to stare at lemons that rot beside grocery store aisles,
And I want to think about happiness like she's a fever dream.
I want to be covered and colored in the hues of grief,

I want to be who I am,
Broken and damaged and crawling back to a whole
I don't fully understand.
I don't like what home tastes like,
But I like the taste of lemons,
And I like the taste of grief.
I just want to create a home,
One nestled safely amidst the brightness,
Layered with colors that refuse to lay obscure
amongst these everyday shades of Brown.

The Suburban Doll House

I wonder if you see my clenched fists,
Hidden beneath this teak table.
As you sit in your chair,
Smug and warm, smiling against a well built bare brick wall,
The gall you have makes me want to choke on my drink,
But then, who are you going to call?
Is it the doctor in the mint green building?
The same one you stabbed tonight?
Or the town physician that's rotting three roads down,
Buried in the town mine?

As you bite your lip,
I remember the time you bit his and called it a lover's quarrel.
Some scars don't heal with time.
They disappear instead mother,
Lost to the naked eye.
But my mind remembers,
And a million fake dinners in beautifully done dining rooms,
Won't begin to replace the promises you broke.

Pray tell mother,
Who will the next victim be?

As I look down at our marbled floors,
I wonder what stories lay buried beneath.
All these pristine gleaming layers.
Why would you make them shine with bleach?
Is it to wipe out the smell of conflict?
The men that lost their lives here?
The ground was meant to be worn out,
Kicks it's destined to receive.
But you're putting up a dangerous illusion mother,
Mirrors always do shatter, in the end that's all that will matter.

Maybe someday I'll take out our Yellow shovel,
Another piece in this perfect suburban puzzle.
A garden shed decorated with weapons, you've veiled many a neighbour blind.
As I dig through this fortress you've constructed
Maybe a man in a blue suit I'll find, jilted by his green eyed lover,
After months and months of pursuit.

Numerous highwaymen,
Shrouded in crimson.
Blood reeks of wasted coins and stained currency mother,

No amount of bleach can corrode that.
But it's the smell of melancholy you're mistaking for the dead.
Friendships lost to clocks that have long stopped ticking,
Have perished in these floors.
As the lights turn off and the dishes are washed,
And the night air lulls everyone to sleep,
The song of the past is sung louder then mother,
Piercing through the veils you've hung over reality.

Can you hear it over your loud parlour music?
The blues of your curtains,
The reds of the velvets you've made chairs with?
The song of mundanity.
Your secrets have been buried for far too long,
They're pulsating with need.
About to tear through the fabric you so carefully picked out,
The upholstery is about to be freed.

They will come home to you,
They're yours to keep.
They will knock on your door,
Break it down if necessary.
Those chairs will crumple under the weight of their pain,

Your upholstery will be stained.
Save your precious trinkets
They're about to break.
As they fall through the floor,
And we run to the door,
Do you wish to patch your dollhouse back up?

Dust off the shelves,
And throw away the bile stained clothes?
Your home reeks of lies mother.
As you clean on a casual Sunday evening,
Think of the lives you left behind.

One day you're an assassin,
Clothed in black,
Hidden by the night, as sharp as midnight's eye.
You're a burglar the next,
Sneaking into the houses of the men that love you,
Lips painted an unbearable flame red.

You suck them dry and leave knives in their palates.
Then you come at night and eat cheeses to cleanse yours.
You pour yourself wine,
Yet every supper you left was cursed to be someone's last.

Running your fingers down my hair,
Pinching my cheeks every now and then,
I'm just another teenager, that's trapped in the devil's lair.

You dressed me up in corduroys and flare pants,
Only the best a parent could provide.
But all those missed meetings, and bring your parent to school days,
I wonder about the tears you produced at the wakes.
Each time a family cried over an empty casket,
You buried a new one in our garden.
You're a cold blooded monster mother,
That's not a profession.
But you call yourself invincible in those thigh highs,
And that's an illusion the world finds hard to shun.

You brought us out for milkshakes and burgers,
But I see your eyes wondering,
You can't hide from me.
You're looking for the next back to carve your knife into,
These walls could be painted with the colours of your hatred,
A blinding ivory.

You act on whims and show no mercy,
But I see through this Jet black facade.
You're hiding behind those sunglasses,
The same ones you smuggled in the prison yard.

My mother is an interesting woman,
I sometimes say with falsely fashioned pride.
My mother is an interesting woman to say the least,
And the very least is what she'll say.
A poem I've learnt like the back of my hand,
Spewing it at every unaware prisoner that enters our home.
They don't understand the nature of the love they've signed up for,
It's an illusory doom.

The picnics we've laughed at and the meats we've roasted,
They've been paid for with money drenched in blood.
My mother is an entrepreneur I say with pride,
Little do they know she deals souls in dimes.

Despite the rosary that's wrapped around your neck.
You're a beast in sheep's clothing mother.
Never have there been wools more tasteful than the ones you wear.

But fleece is a mortal cover mother,
You'll soon find yourself uncloaked.
For judgement day comes for everyone,
Even assassins armed with guns.
You can't fire at the darkness mother,
She's the force and the fog that consumes
whatever runs.

Push and shove and see what gives,
Maybe someday it'll be me.
I'll spill the truth on these white walls you've built.
They'll be stained by the tricks your hand has dealt.

You scatter blood like it's ichor,
Curse at it like its poison,
But your walls are made of brick too mother,
Someday they'll crash and burn.
Much like the cars you've stood in front of,
Waving a dainty arm,
But scarves don't hide the scars you have on your
soul mother,
They'll show themselves someday.

A white cottage and pink curtains,
Freshly manicured lawns and detailed edges,
Not a hair out of place.
Neatly arranging your ponytail, pinning it back up
with lace.
Congratulations,

You've built a farce even you can't fully see through,
Its been put exactly in its place.
We watch TV in the evenings and microwave
dinners freely,
But there's bodies behind these walls, mother.
How many incense sticks will you sacrifice?
How many more men will suffice?

You have all the money and the perfect brick house,
But what are you going to do about your cold dead
heart?
Beat it on the ground and restore it back to life?

Cruelty is your elixir, isn't it mother?
You feed it to the lost and the living,
But what will you do when these bricks corrode?
Will your doll house still be your abode?

Acknowledgements

If you made it this far, I would like to start by acknowledging you for your patience and for sticking with me to the end. Writing this book hasn't been an easy experience and there are multiple people I would like to thank for their love, kindness and grace. Starting with, my parents and my dearest grandfather, thank you for supporting my dreams and my ambitions, my love for you knows no bounds. To my friends who are now family, thank you for reading all my poems and for giving me ruthless yet incredibly constructive feedback, I love you.

And finally, to K, thank you for your unending feedback and the endless hours you've sat reading my poetry. I love you.

www.ingramcontent.com/pod-product-compliance
Lightning Source LLC
La Vergne TN
LVHW091117150826
845673LV00002B/877

* 9 7 9 8 8 9 2 7 7 3 4 0 9 *